BACKPACK 5

Mario Herrera   **Diane Pinkley**

Contents

Backpack Song

It's time to open **Backpack**
   and see what we can see.
We'll have lots of adventures.
Explore **Backpack** with me!

Backpack is full of fun things
   we use each day in school.
Stories, puzzles, songs, and games--
Backpack is really cool!

It's time to open **Backpack**
   and see what we can see.
We'll have lots of adventures.
Explore **Backpack** with me!

Backpack is full of fun and facts,
   projects and pictures, too.
We're learning English, we're never bored.
There are great new things to do!

It's time to open **Backpack**
   and see what we can see.
We'll have lots of adventures.
Explore **Backpack** with me!

The Family Circle

Who's there?

1 Read. Listen and sing.

A Surprise Visit

It was just about a quarter to four,
when I heard a knock on my front door.
I looked outside and what did I see?
Ten pairs of eyes looking back at me!

My favorite cousins all were there,
and Grandma Jones with her long gray hair;
my uncle Tito and auntie Ru
with all their kids, including Sue.

Angela's taller than Ben, I see,
and curly-haired Pat is as cute as can be.
Uncle Mark is letting his beard grow longer.
David looks so much bigger and stronger.

Everyone ate and drank and stayed until ten,
gave me a hug, and said, "See you again!"
But I don't mind at all, you see,
because they're my loving family.

2 Listen and read.

Dear Jenny,

We had a wonderful family reunion in the park. I was so sorry to hear that you were sick and couldn't come! I missed my favorite niece, and everyone says hello. Well, now for the details. Grandpa and Grandma Jones brought presents for all the grandchildren. Your uncle Mark now has a beard. Your auntie Ru got new glasses. When it was time to eat, uncle Tito cooked veggie burgers and hot dogs on the grill. Aunt Gina made that horrible broccoli salad, and as usual, no one ate it! Most of the kids played soccer or listened to your cousin Jack play his guitar. And, of course, we laughed a lot, told stories, and took lots of pictures!

Love,

Aunt Sophie

We had a wonderful time!

3 Talk and stick.

4 Look and read.

Here's Joy's scrapbook about the Iglesias family.

Enrique, my favorite singer, was born in May, the same month I was! He is the cutest of Julio and Isabel's three children.

Here I am in line for the concert! I waited for hours to get in! I was so excited!

Enrique's brother Julio José is also a singer. He tried modeling and acting, too. Julio Jr. is younger than his sister Chabeli, but older than Enrique. He is really good-looking.

María Isabel, also called Chabeli, is the oldest. She looks a lot like her mother. She is married and has one son, Alejandro. He is Enrique's nephew.

Julio Iglesias, Enrique's dad, is a famous singer. He played soccer for Real Madrid in Spain before he started singing. I think he's a handsome man. He holds a world record for sales of over 250 million albums.

Isabel Preysler, Enrique's mom, was born in the Philippines. She's very beautiful. I can't believe she is a grandmother. She looks so young.

⑤ Point. Ask and answer.

What does he look like?

He's good-looking, with dark hair and dark eyes.

⑥ Ask and answer.

Who is the youngest, Julio José, Enrique, or Chabeli?

Enrique is the youngest.

My grandparents are great! They gave me <u>all</u> of Enrique's CDs!

Grammar

> Julio José is **older than** Enrique.
> Chabeli is **older than** Julio José.
> Chabeli is **the oldest** of the three.

7 **Write complete sentences.**

Eric, 10

Monica, 12

Carlos, 15

1. Who is shorter than Monica?

   Eric is shorter than Monica. _____

2. Who is the oldest?

   _____

3. Who is younger than Monica?

   _____

4. Who is older, Monica or Carlos?

   _____

5. Who is the tallest?

   _____

Grammar

> There **was** a long line for the concert.
> I **waited** in line for a long time.
> I **had** a wonderful time at the concert.

8 **Complete the sentences. Use the past tense.**

1. Enrique Iglesias ____was____ born in Madrid, Spain.

2. He _____ up in Miami, Florida.

3. He _____ business in school before singing.

4. He _____ his first album in 1995.

5. He _____ a Grammy award for his album *Vivir*.

be
grow
make
study
win

9 What does your family
look like? Ask and answer.

aunt	cousin	grandmother	sister
brother	grandfather	nephew/niece	uncle

Hair	Eyes	Body	Face	Appearance
curly	black	average	freckles	beautiful
long	blue	heavy		good-looking
short	brown	thin	beard	handsome
straight	green	short	mustache	pretty
wavy		tall		
	glasses			
black	contacts	strong		
blond				
brown				
gray				
red				

What does your
aunt look like?

She's tall and thin.
She has wavy brown hair
and freckles. She
wears contacts.

Aunt Rose

10 Talk about yourself and your family.
Ask and answer.

1. When and where were you born?

2. Where did you grow up?

3. How many brothers and sisters do you have?

4. In your family, who is the youngest?

5. In your family, who is older than you?

I was born in Puebla,
but I grew up in
Monterrey.

Where were
you born?

E-Pals International

The Magazine for Electronic Pen Pals Around the World

IN THIS ISSUE:
Focus on Our Readers

Chi-young Park was born in the port city of Busan, Korea but she grew up in Seoul with her grandparents, mother, father, brother, and sister. Chi-young wanted to be a musician until last year, but now she wants to be a computer engineer like her father. She spends a lot of time at her computer, sending messages to Alberto and other e-pals around the world. Chi-young loves dancing, music, and her mother's delicious moon cakes!

Chi-young Park

Today's E-Joke

Student: Teacher, would you please e-mail my exam results to my parents?

Teacher: But your parents don't have a computer.

Student: Exactly!

Chi-young sent Alberto an e-mail at 7:00 A.M. on Tuesday, but Alberto got it at 5:00 P.M. on Monday, the day before she sent it! How is this possible?

Alberto Valenzuela

Visit these websites with your teacher

www.epals.com

www.iecc.org

www.ipfs.org

Be an Electronic Pen Pal!

Make new friends all over the world.

Alberto Valenzuela was born in Guadalajara, Mexico. He lives there with his uncle, aunt, and three cousins. Right now, Alberto thinks he wants to be an art teacher, like his aunt Dolores. He loves to play soccer and draw pictures of his family and friends. At school, Alberto's favorite subject is computer science. That's when he gets to write e-mail and find out all the news from Chi-young and his other pen pals around the world.

This is me!

Alberto

Learn a new language!

English	Spanish	Korean	Esperanto
mom	mamá	umma	patrino
dad	papá	appa	patro
brother	hermano	hyung	frato
sister	hermana	nunah	fratino

Listen. Write the letter.

1. Emma __e__
2. Kirk _____
3. Joan _____
4. Sammy _____
5. Gloria _____

 a

 b

OUR FAMILY CIRCLE

 c

 d

 e

 Listen. Read and chant.

Family Album

I love to take a certain album
from its special shelf,
brush it off and open it up
to photos of myself.
There I am with my parents,
when I was only three.
And here I am with cousin Ken,
in the tallest apple tree.
And there I am on my first bike,
riding really fast,
and here's the photo my uncle took,
my left arm is in a cast.
Here's the day I made the goal
for our soccer victory.
And there I am with my dad,
who was so proud of me.

Project

Family History

Make a poster about your grandparents.

And this is my Grandma Hisako. She was born in Kobe, Japan. She met my grandfather at school. They were teachers there.

My Grandparents

Grandfather Mitsue a teacher.

Grandma Hisako was a teacher. She was born in Kobe, Japan.

Grandfather Hiro was a businessman. He was born in Osaka, Japan.

Grandma Junko was a housewife. She was born in Osaka, Japan.

Play a Game!

Cut out the cards on page 113.

grandfather	cousin	sister
grandmother	nephew	uncle
niece	aunt	mother

This is your father's father.

I know this one! Grandfather.

And last is Uncle Amir. He always has a good story to tell.

✓ **KNOW IT? SHOW IT!**

Talk about your family circle.

Uncle David   **Fernando**   **Alicia**

✔ **Look at the pictures. Complete the sentences.**

1. Alicia has the _____ hair.

2. Fernando wears _____.

3. Uncle David is _____ than Fernando.

4. Alicia is the _____.

5. Uncle David has dark, _____ hair.

✔ **Complete the sentences. Use the past tense.**

1. Marta _____ born in the month of February.

2. Tony _____ up in a small town.

3. He _____ to the city when he was seven.

4. My cousin Jack _____ the guitar for two hours.

5. Aunt Gina _____ her awful broccoli salad.

| be |
| grow |
| make |
| move |
| play |

Write about your favorite family member.

1. What does he or she look like?

2. What does he or she do?

3. Why is this person your favorite family member?

_____

_____

_____

_____

_____

What's on TV?

1 Read. Listen and sing.

TV Time

Say, what is on TV tonight?
Does anybody know?
I feel like watching a movie
or maybe a nature show.

I don't mind a good comedy,
like the one with the talking plane.
Or maybe you can sit with me
to watch a soccer game.

I like to watch the news sometimes,
or maybe an action cartoon.
I really like science fiction shows
with aliens from the moon.

Then there's the cooking channel
with lots of tasty treats.
And for music I watch MTV
to hear the latest beats.

And then there's drama and mystery,
and always a new game show.
So what is on TV tonight?
Doesn't anybody know?

What's your favorite show?

Listen. Read and say.

TV3 : Do you watch a lot of TV?

Dan: Yeah. I watch TV every day. I usually watch cartoons and sports.

TV3: And what about you?

Pat: I like to do other things, like play outside and ride my bike. I watch TV about once a week.

TV3: Just once? What do you watch?

Pat: I always watch the Friday night mystery movie on channel 7 with my family.

TV3: And you? How much TV do you watch?

Bill: I watch a lot of sports, but only on weekends. I don't watch TV during the week.

TV3: OK, your turn. Do you like to watch TV?

Kim: Yes. I watch my favorite comedy show twice a week, on Tuesday and Thursday.

TV3: How often do you watch TV?

Sue: About three times a month, when I visit my aunt. We don't have a TV at home!

3 **Talk and stick.**

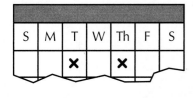

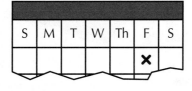

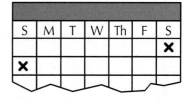

Television is a favorite form of entertainment around the world. TV networks show different types of programs on their channels.

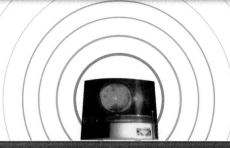

Reality Shows

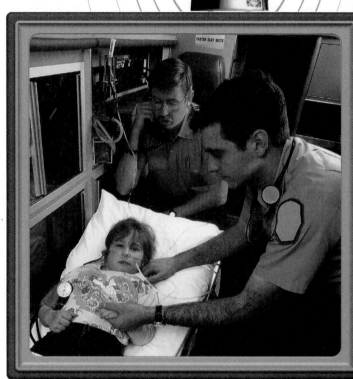

In this kind of program, TV cameras film live events as they happen. The people in the program are not actors, and they do not follow a written script or story. Some reality shows may film teenagers living away from home or people surviving on an isolated island. Other reality shows film firefighters, police officers, or emergency medical teams as they answer calls for help. Still others follow young people as they try to become famous models, actors, dancers, or singers. Reality shows can be very exciting and dramatic.

Talk Shows

On some talk shows, a host and several guests discuss serious topics such as politics, health, or the environment. On other talk shows, different people from daily life explain their personal problems to the program host and audience. The host and the people in the audience often give advice or make comments. The problems and the comments can be sad, funny, or shocking, but they are always interesting.

Soap Operas

These daytime and nighttime dramas can be exciting, sad, romantic, suspenseful, and funny—sometimes all in the same episode! The characters are usually members of large families, and TV viewers follow everything that happens to them as they leave home, get jobs, fall in love, and get into trouble of different kinds.

News

Most people like to watch an evening news program to find out what happened during the day in their town, in their country, and around the world. They can also learn about local weather and sports. News programs are usually interesting and informative.

5 Point. Ask and answer.

What kind of TV shows do you like?

I like reality shows. I think they're exciting.

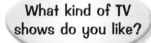

6 Ask and answer.

How often do you watch reality shows?

About three or four times a week.

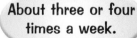

What kind of TV shows **do** you **like**?   I **like** reality shows.
I **think** they're exciting.

Dan **doesn't like** talk shows.   He **thinks** they're boring.

7 **Look and write. Use *like* and *think*.**

cartoon   cooking show   soap opera   sports

1. I ___like_____ . I think _____ .

2. Anne _____ . _____ .

3. I _____ . _____ .

4. Luke _____ . _____ .

Grammar

How often do you watch reality shows? I watch reality shows **once a week**.
My sister watches them   ⎫ **twice a week**.
My friend Julia watches them ⎬ **four times a week**.
My brother watches them   ⎭ **on weekends**.

8 **Write questions and answers.**

1. How often do you watch the news on TV?

_____

2. _____
I never watch science fiction shows.

3. How often do you watch game shows?

_____

4. _____
Jennifer watches talk shows twice a month.

What's on TV at 10:00?

A game show called 'Your Turn.' It's on channel 4. I think it's a fun show.

9 **Work with a partner.**

Student A uses this information.
Student B turns to page 110.

TV This Week	Saturday A.M.		
	Channel 2	**Channel 4**	**Channel 6**
10:00	*Kids Can Cook* cooking show (30 min.)	*Your Turn* game show (60 min.)	
10:30			*Crazy Daisy* comedy (60 min.)
11:00	*News for Kids* news show (60 min.)		
11:30		*In the Money* game show (60 min.)	
12:00			*Space Wars* science fiction (2 hrs.)

10 **Write. Then talk about your favorite TV shows in a group.**

	Show Title	Time	Channel	Show Type	Characters
1.					
2.					
3.					

TV Talk
The Magazine All About TV

Our Readers Report

Fifth-grade Students Learn TV Production

The Japan Broadcasting Corporation (NHK) helped over 600 lucky fifth and sixth graders learn all about the basics of producing television programs. Students from nine schools visited the Osaka TV station to learn how to operate cameras, lights, and sound equipment. Students also wrote scripts and produced their own videos about their school districts. The videos show news programs about local school and community events. Some of the children acted as newscasters, others as floor directors, and others as technicians. They all enjoyed the experience and learned a lot. Check your local TV station to see if there are programs for you!

Are YOU a Couch Potato?

Send us your answers and find out.

1. How many hours do you watch TV each week?

2. How often do you say *no* to friends to stay home and watch your favorite programs?

3. How often do you eat your meals with the TV on?

4. How often do you fall asleep with the TV on?

5. How often do you turn on the TV right after you get home from school?

A couch potato watches too much TV.

The Science Corner

How Do Televisions Work?

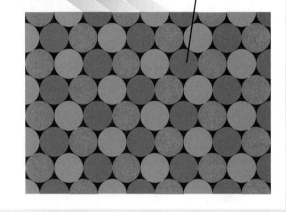

Three guns create colors—red, blue, and green.

Small holes in a mask guide each gun's "bullets" so that they can only hit the correct color dot on the TV screen.

Each gun hits the right red, blue, or green dot and makes it glow.

Inside your TV is a special "gun" that "shoots" a constant stream of electrically charged particles like bullets. When the particles hit the TV screen, they make it glow. The TV picture is made up of many thousands of glowing dots.

Take the TV Challenge!

Complete the puzzle with TV-related words.

```
r  e  m  o  t  e      c  o  n  t  r  o  l
                                        m
      v                 c        l      d
                        h        s
      t                 p
      y      i
      h      o                   a
      w      n
```

NEXT MONTH!

Satellite Dish or Cable?

11 **Listen. Write the number.**

 12 **Listen. Read and chant.**

THE REMOTE

Oh, no, how could this happen?
My program starts at three.
I need to find the remote control
and change channels on TV.

Will I be forced to leave this couch
and look around the room?
Where in the world is my remote?
The game's beginning soon!

It's not between the cushions,
or buried in the crack.
My program's starting in a second.
I want my clicker back!

Now I'm feeling something
in the pillow behind my head.
There it is! I'm saved at last!
Oh, no, the battery's dead!

SOCIAL STUDIES

TV Viewing Habits

Make a chart.

TV Viewing Habits

Name	Do you watch TV every day?	Do you watch TV more during the week or on the weekend?	What is your favorite kind of program?
1. Marcia	✓	on weekends	cooking shows
2. Ken	✓	on weekends	sports
3. Jee-Wha	✓	weekdays	soap operas
4. Cynthia	✓	on weekends	movies
		on weekends	nature shows
		on weekends	sports
7. Susan	✓	on weekends	cartoons
8. David	✓	on weekends	cartoons
9. Khalid	✓	weekdays	game shows
10. Alicia	✓	on weekends	reality shows

I interviewed 10 people. All of them watch some TV every day. They usually watch more TV on weekends.

PLaY a GaMe!

Cut out the pictures on page 115.

 In this show, you learn about local events, weather, and sports.

 The news!

Yes! It's your turn.

My favorite show is 'Nature Hour.' It's on channel 9 at 3:00 every Saturday afternoon. I think it's exciting, especially when they show snakes.

 KNOW IT? SHOW IT!

Make a collage about your favorite TV show.

Write words.

1. _____ 2. _____ 3. _____ 4. _____

Read and complete the sentences.

	Show Type	How Often He/She Watches
John	nature shows	Monday, Thursday
Kim	soap operas	Monday, Tuesday, Wednesday, Thursday, Friday, Saturday, Sunday
Gloria	comedy shows	Tuesday, Thursday, Saturday
Bill	sports	Saturday, Sunday
June	cooking shows	Wednesday

every day
once a week
on weekends
three times a week
twice a week

1. John _____

2. Kim _____

3. Gloria _____

4. Bill _____

5. June _____

Write about one of your favorite TV shows.

_____

_____

_____

_____

Hands On

Handmade

I could take a lump of clay
and make a crocodile.
I would give it bumpy skin
and a scary smile.

I could take a brush and paint
a scene that's sure to please,
of bushes, grass, and flowers,
and blooming cherry trees.

I could take some blocks of wood
and build a wooden bench.
I'd need to use a screwdriver,
a hammer, and a wrench.

I could take some cotton cloth
and make something to wear.
I would make a pair of pants
and sew them up with care.

I could use my hands to make
anything—it's true.
Making things is lots of fun.
You should try it, too!

2 **Listen. Read and say.**

Chin: Hi, Fran. What are you going to make for your art project?

Fran: I'm not sure. I have two ideas.

Chin: What's the first idea?

Fran: I could set up an easel outdoors and paint a picture of the school.

Chin: That sounds like fun.

Fran: Or I could carve a design on a block of wood and make block prints.

Chin: Oh, that idea's even better.

Fran: I can't decide what to do. What are you going to do?

Chin: I could make a sculpture out of wire. My father has a lot of copper wire that he doesn't need.

Fran: That sounds interesting.

Chin: Or I could make a model of a bridge out of wood.

Fran: Those are both great ideas!

3 **Talk and stick.**

What could Fran and Chin make?

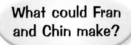

4 Look and read.

People around the world enjoy arts and crafts.

Mercedes enjoys weaving. Her grandmother taught her how to weave when she was just seven years old. Mercedes weaves by hand, using the traditional Guatemalan loom that her mother and her grandmother used. Mercedes uses brightly colored yarns to make beautiful cloths. Weaving is an important Guatemalan tradition, and Mercedes is proud to be part of that tradition.

Liang likes painting. He paints in the traditional Chinese style, using special brushes, ink, and paper. He practices his brushstroke by painting the same thing, such as a rooster, again and again. In this style of painting, a few simple brushstrokes have to suggest a lot of detail. The wrong brushstroke could ruin a picture. Traditional Chinese painting is not easy, but it's exciting.

Lorenzo loves carving. He carves animals and imaginary creatures out of wood and paints them bright colors. This style of carving is called *alebrije*, a Zapotec Indian word meaning "fantastic" or "imaginary." Lorenzo learned how to carve from his father, an *alebrije* artist. *Alebrije* carving isn't an old tradition. It is recent. It's only about 20 years old, yet it is already popular in many different parts of the world.

Ramona enjoys knitting. She makes socks, hats, and sweaters using a soft yarn made from alpaca wool. Alpacas are animals that look like llamas. Most of the alpacas in the world live in Peru, where Ramona lives. Knitting clothes is one way Peruvian women can make a living.

5 Point. Ask and answer.

What craft does Mercedes enjoy?

Mercedes enjoys weaving.

6 Ask and answer.

What do you know about weaving?

Weaving is an important Guatemalan tradition.

Grammar

Gerund Subject	Gerund Object
Sewing your own clothes saves you money.	Anita enjoys **sewing** her own clothes.
Drawing is Jin's favorite hobby.	Jin likes **drawing** pictures of imaginary creatures.

7 **Complete the sentences.**

carve
knit
paint
weave

1. _____ with a loom is an important business in Japan and other countries.

2. Don likes _____ animal figures out of wood.

3. _____ with watercolors is a lot of fun.

4. I enjoy _____ pairs of mittens for people in my family.

Grammar

What **could** Rita and Marcos do for their mother's birthday?
They **could** bake a cake for her.

8 **Answer the questions.**

1. How could Lisa spend a rainy Saturday? (sew her jeans)
   She could sew her jeans.

2. What could we cook for dinner? (make spaghetti)
   _____

3. How could you fill an empty sheet of paper? (draw a picture)
   _____

4. What could Maya do with yarn? (knit a hat)
   _____

5. What could Diego do with these fresh vegetables? (make a salad)
   _____

9 Interview your classmates.
Find a different student for each picture.

Ken, do you enjoy painting pictures?

Yes. Painting with watercolors is a lot of fun.

 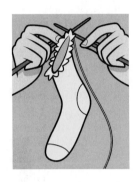  

 Ken

10 Talk to your classmates.

What crafts do you like?

I like woodworking because you use tools like saws, drills, hammers, and screwdrivers.

This Kid Can Cook!

Lauren Assayag, a fifth grader from California, won $10,000 in a kids' recipe contest. Lauren's recipe for Mango Avocado Chicken Strips won the grand prize out of 403 entries. The judges liked Lauren's recipe best because it was the tastiest, healthiest, and easiest to make of all the recipes in the contest. Lauren was proud because she made up the recipe herself. What will she do with the $10,000? She loves cooking, so she plans to go to cooking school. Lauren could be a famous chef one day!

Look, Mom, No Hands!

Painting may be a hands-on activity, but some elephants do very well with their trunks! Why are these elephants painting? Believe it or not, painting is their new job. Long ago, people used elephants to carry logs from rain forests. After too many rain forests were destroyed, logging was stopped. No one needed the elephants anymore. When artists Vitaly Komar and Alex Melamid heard about these unwanted elephants, they decided to teach the animals how to paint. People began to buy the elephants' paintings. The money from the paintings helps support the elephants.

Weaving with Paper

Make a place mat or a basket!

Step 1: Fold a sheet of paper in half.

Step 2: Make cuts from the fold to the edges. Leave about an inch (2.54 cm) between each cut and stop cutting about two inches (5.0 cm) from the edge. Your cuts can be straight or curved.

Step 3: Unfold the paper.

Step 4: Cut strips of colored paper.

Step 5: Weave the paper strips into the paper with the cuts. Be sure to alternate the over and under motion for each strip.

Step 6: Glue the ends of the strips to the edges of the paper.

Word Search

brushes	cooking	loom	weaving
carving	drawing	paints	wood
clay	knitting	sewing	yarn

```
P E D C V R S O J A S E W I N G
I U R U S E I Y A R N F E B C E
C L A Y N L B L U X E R A C H U
E O W O O D H U N C A R V I N G
S O I S L E I P O G I K I T O H
D M N B I R K A R C T S N E T F
A F G Y Q K N I T T I N G S A L
I U S C U E R N O Y N U F E R I
C O O K I N G T L J T E R L E C
E R L O S V H S N B R U S H E S
```

NEXT WEEK

Making Model Cars

11 Listen. Write the letter.

1. _____
2. _____
3. _____
4. _____
5. _____

a

b

c

d

e

12 Listen. Read and chant.

Crafty Kids

Carla has new watercolors.
She likes painting cats.
Pat loves knitting woolly things
like sweaters, socks, and hats.

> Nardo's always busy with his
> potter's wheel and clay.
> Making clothes is fun for Kim.
> It's how she spends each day.

Marisol likes carving things
out of soap or wood.
Playing music on his flute
makes Anthony feel good.

> You could choose an art or craft—
> something right for you.
> Just as long as you enjoy
> doing what you do.

Project

Crafts Around the Globe

Make a class book.

I love folding paper into animal shapes.

Folding paper into shapes takes practice.

PLay a GaMe!

Cut out the cards on page 117.

✓ KNOW IT? SHOW IT!

Talk with your classmates about a craft you enjoy.

✔ Write words.

1. _____ 2. _____ 3. _____ 4. _____ 5. _____

✔ Complete the sentences.

1. Hea makes sweaters using needles and yarn. She enjoys _____.

2. My brothers have guitars. _____ music is their hobby.

3. _____ has a long history in Guatemala.

4. Sandra doesn't like _____, but she likes drawing.

5. _____ your own clothes is a good way to save money.

✔ Answer the questions.

1. What could you do with clay?

_____

2. What could you do with paper, paint, and a brush?

_____

3. What could you make with a needle, thread, and cloth?

_____

What are some interesting crafts you enjoy?

_____

_____

_____

_____

I'll Take It!

1 Read. Listen and sing.

At the Outdoor Market

When Mom and I go shopping,
it's a very exciting day.
We visit an outdoor market
that runs along the bay.

Anything we want or need
is somewhere in a stall.
From food to clothes to new CDs,
our market has it all.

The stalls I love to visit
have the most colorful clothes.
I see flowers, stripes, and checks
hanging high in rows.

We buy the most delicious fruit
at my favorite stall.
And next door are the new CDs
by the most popular groups of all.

We always leave too exhausted
to walk home from the train.
But the next time my mother wants to,
I'm ready to shop again.

Listen. Read and say.

Lucia: So what do you think of this jacket? Are the sleeves too short?

Paolo: Yes. They aren't long enough.

Carlos: And what about this shirt? How do you think it fits?

Lucia: The colors are great, but I think it's too tight.

Paolo: Yeah. I like the stripes, but that shirt isn't big enough.

Carlos: OK. I'll look for a larger size.

Paolo: And this cap is just right. I'll take it!

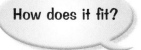

How does it fit?

3 **Talk and stick.**

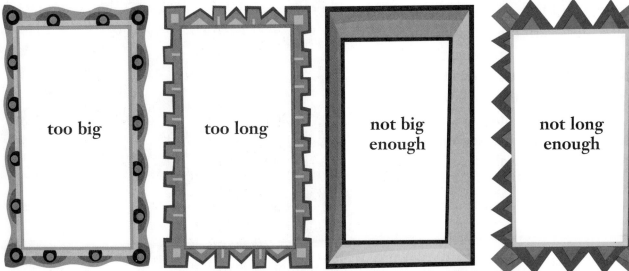

too big

too long

not big enough

not long enough

4 Look and read.

Every country in the world has outdoor markets, sometimes called street markets.

Do you go to a supermarket or to an open-air market to do your shopping? You can find the most amazing merchandise in an outdoor market right next to typical everyday items. Outdoor markets are exciting places full of noise, color, smells, and busy shoppers. Sometimes the crowds are too big, but everyone enjoys shopping just the same.

The bird section of an outdoor market is colorful and noisy. You can find all kinds of birds for sale. The birds with the most beautiful songs are more expensive than the birds that sing just a few notes. Bird owners take their birds out of their cages and walk them around the market. You can see them feed the birds meals of insects and small worms!

In the jewelry section of a market, you can find necklaces, bracelets, earrings, rings, and even gemstones. Gold jewelry is more expensive than silver jewelry. If you see something you want, name a price a little lower than you want to pay, and keep bargaining until the price is not too high. Getting a good bargain is the most exciting part of all!

5 **Ask and answer.**

Which markets are more exciting— supermarkets or outdoor markets?

Outdoor markets.

6 **Ask and answer.**

What is the most interesting section of the market?

For me, the clothing section, because I like comparing styles and prices.

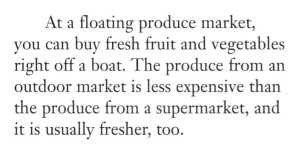

At a floating produce market, you can buy fresh fruit and vegetables right off a boat. The produce from an outdoor market is less expensive than the produce from a supermarket, and it is usually fresher, too.

Grammar

Outdoor markets are **interesting**.

Outdoor markets are **more interesting than** supermarkets.

Outdoor markets are **the most interesting** places to shop.

7 **Complete the sentence. Use** *more . . . than* **or** *the most.*

1. The silver jewelry is _____ the beaded jewelry.
(beautiful)

2. Outdoor markets have _____ clothes of all.
(colorful)

3. Birds with beautiful songs are _____ of all.
(expensive)

4. The items at an outdoor market are often _____
the items in a supermarket. (unusual)

5. Getting a good bargain is _____ part of shopping
at an outdoor market. (exciting)

Grammar

The price of that necklace is **too** high.   The price isn't low **enough**.

These shoes are **too** small.   These shoes aren't big **enough**.

| beautiful | big | colorful | expensive | high |
| long | ~~low~~ | new | small | unusual |

~~birdcage~~
CDs
jacket
necklace
shirt
shoes

8 **Write sentences. Use** *too* **or** *enough* **and a word from
each box.**

1. The price of that birdcage isn't low enough.

2. _____

3. _____

4. _____

5. _____

9 Work with a partner.

Student A uses this information to ask and answer questions.
Student B turns to page 110.

Discount Dave's
★★★
We have everything!
Check out these low, low prices!

$45.00

$129.95

$8.50

$17.00

Super discounts every Thursday!

Stacy's
Department Store

BIG SALE _____

Jewelry

$_____

$135.00

Sweaters

$_____

Footwear

$89.95

10 Talk to your classmates about the ads.

Those are the most popular sneakers now. And the price isn't too high.

I like the red sweater. It's more fashionable than the others.

That gold necklace is too expensive.

The Shopper's Stall
the magazine all about shopping

The Shopper's Stall Presents . . .
short story by our reader Graciela Hernandez

After Hours

Is it more fun to be in a store when it is open or closed?

Read and decide!

Grace stood by the door of the dressing room holding a pile of clothes. "I don't believe this!" she finally said out loud. The store was closed. How long was she trying on clothes in the dressing room this afternoon? What time was it now? Why didn't anyone find her?

She left the clothes on a counter and then checked her backpack. Her cell phone was not inside. Grace walked to a pay phone near the store entrance, but it was out of order. Then she sighed and looked around her. The store was quiet and empty.

Hey, she thought suddenly. This doesn't have to be a *bad* thing. Someone will find me. Until they do, the whole store is *mine*. I can try on all the clothes I want!

Grace went upstairs where the most expensive clothes were sold. She smiled as she saw the rows of designer jeans, dresses, and leather jackets.

Then, all of a sudden, she heard the sound of breaking glass on the first floor. Was someone in the store? Grace hid behind a row of coats. She almost screamed as every light in the store went out.

continued in next week's issue . . .

Spotlight On: Flashing Light Jewelry

Do you want people to notice you? Then you might want to buy earrings, necklaces, or rings that light up and flash on and off!

How is this possible? It's all due to a phenomenon called electroluminescence, but you don't have to be a scientist to understand it. All you need to know is that small batteries provide the energy needed to make the jewelry light up and blink on and off. Wear this fashionable jewelry to parties, or even every day. We promise you will amaze your friends!

100 QUESTIONS and 100 ANSWERS

This week we asked 100 ten- and eleven-year-old kids what they enjoy shopping for.

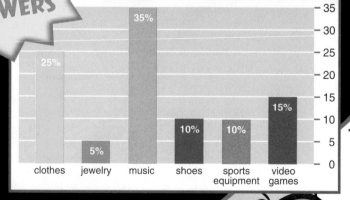

clothes	jewelry	music	shoes	sports equipment	video games
25%	5%	35%	10%	10%	15%

I forgot my money. I am so dumb!

The Customer is Always Right

Laugh It Up!

JOKE OF THE WEEK

Q: What did the tie say to the hat?

A: You take off, and I'll hang around.

11 Listen. Write the letter.

1. ____
2. ____
3. ____
4. ____

a

b

c

d

12 Listen. Read and chant.

Shop 'Til You Drop

We love shopping at the mall.
It really is the best.
There are so many stores to see
there's never time to rest.
Look inside that clothing shop
at all those leather jackets.
We want to buy some video games,
and find some tennis rackets.
We love shopping at the mall
for it has everything,
from books and shoes,
to rock and blues,
or even a diamond ring.

Project

Commercial

Make a commercial for a product.

Tick Tock watches are the most popular watches for kids. If you want to be in style, get a Tick Tock watch today!

PLaY a GaMe!

Cut out the cards on page 119.

KNOW IT? SHOW IT!

Take an object from the grab bag.
Name a price and bargain.

✔ Write words.

1. _____ 2. _____ 3. _____ 4. _____

✔ Write sentences with the same meanings.

1. This shirt isn't big enough.

_____

2. These pants are too short.

_____

3. Jack is too young to shop by himself.

_____

4. The price isn't low enough.

_____

✔ Complete the sentences with *more . . . than* or *the most*.

1. This store is _____ the other one. (interesting)

2. I think this shop has _____ things in town. (unusual)

3. Dina bought _____ dress in the store. (expensive)

4. Salsa Sam's new CD is _____ his last one. (popular)

What do you like to shop for? Why?

_____

_____

_____

_____

Travel Trouble

A Wet Weekend

We went on a trip last weekend.
It was such a beautiful day.
We left the city to see the country,
but got lost along the way.

We drove for endless hours
up dirt roads and down,
with no idea where we were going.
There wasn't even a town!

Then the clouds grew heavy and dark.
A strong wind began to blow.
We could see a storm was coming.
It was time for us to go!

We tried to turn the car around,
but it was all in vain.
Thunder clapped and lightning flashed,
and down came pouring rain.

How we got back home that day,
I will never really know.
But from my worst day I have learned—
on country trips, don't go!

2 Listen and read.

Sunshine Travel Agency

Dear Sir or Madam:

My family and I were driving to the airport at 6:00 a.m. last Saturday when it started to rain. There was terrible traffic on the highway. We called the airline to change to a later flight. Ten minutes later, all traffic stopped and we didn't move an inch for two hours! We finally got to the airport at 9:45 a.m. We missed both flights! We were waiting for a third flight when the same thunderstorm hit the airport. The storm closed down the airport for hours. We had to cancel our plans. Can we change our tickets?

Yours truly,

Alex Gordon

What happened?

3 Talk and stick.

When I went to the beach, the sun was shining. Then it got cloudy. I was swimming when it began to rain. Soon it was pouring! I had to go back to our hotel. It was rainy and chilly for the rest of my vacation! I was very disappointed.

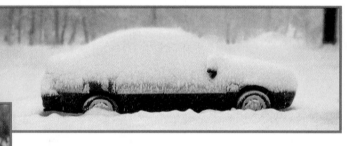

We wanted to go skiing but we couldn't! While we were driving, it got very cold and snowy. We got stuck in the snow! I took this photo while we were waiting for help.

My sister and I love to go on fishing trips. Last year, we were fishing on our favorite lake when it suddenly got very windy. The wind was blowing and waves were crashing over our canoe when another fisherman in a big boat rescued us. We were lucky!

Here is my best picture of the Golden Gate Bridge in San Francisco. It was so foggy that I couldn't take any good photos! The one day it was sunny I forgot my camera. While I was running back to the hotel to get it, I fell and broke my ankle! It was the worst vacation of my life!

5 Point. Ask and answer.

What was he doing when it began to rain?

He was swimming.

6 Ask and answer.

What happened while he was swimming?

It began to rain.

Grammar

Was he **swimming** when it began to rain? Yes, he **was**.
No, he **wasn't**.

Were they **waiting** at the airport all day? Yes, they **were**.
No, they **weren't**.

7 **Complete the sentences.**

1. _____ Jane _____ (take) photos when it began to rain?

   Yes, _____.

2. _____ Joe and Ed _____ (walk) to school at 8:15 this morning?

   Yes, _____.

3. _____ Grace _____ (do) her homework at 9:00 p.m.?

   No, _____.

4. _____ Tony and Nick _____ (watch) TV when the lights went out?

   No, _____.

Grammar

What **was** she **doing** <u>when</u> it began to rain?
She **was walking** the dog <u>when</u> it began to rain.

What happened <u>while</u> they **were riding** their bikes?
It began to rain <u>while</u> they **were riding** their bikes.

8 **Write questions or answers.**

1. What was Bill doing when the telephone rang?

   _____

2. _____

   Mary was reading a book when the lights went out.

3. What happened while they were waiting at the airport?

   _____

4. _____

   It began to snow while they were walking home.

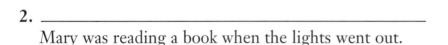

9 How's your memory? Take turns making sentences.

10 Write the names of three classmates.
Complete the sentences about them.

Names	What you think they were doing
Angela	She was eating breakfast at 7:45 this morning.
1. _____	_____ at 8:30 this morning.
2. _____	_____ when the teacher came in.
3. _____	_____ when the teacher asked a question.

Now ask your classmates what they were doing at those times.

Did you guess correctly?
If so, put a check by the name.

Travel Tales Magazine

Tips for a Great Trip!

- Take some books, magazines, and video games for those long waits.
- Take bottled water and some snacks.
- Take extra film for your camera.
- Keep photocopies of your travel papers in two different places.

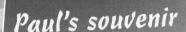

NEXT MONTH
My best travel experience

Our Readers Write Us

Paul's souvenir

My Worst Travel Experience
by Paul Roberts

Last year my parents decided to take my brother Billy and me to a real cowboy ranch for our vacation. I was happy and excited. Soon after I got to the ranch, I went out to see the beautiful horses. I really wanted to learn to ride a horse, and so I climbed on one right away when no one was looking. While I was sitting in the saddle, the horse started moving! I didn't know how to stop it. I held on tightly as the horse began to run. It was so scary! We were running through a field of cactus when the horse saw a snake on the ground. The horse jumped back, and I fell off—right into a big bunch of cactus! I spent hours pulling out cactus thorns. That was the worst experience I ever had! But at least I got a puppy!

Did you know ?

Murphy's Law

When you run into trouble as you travel, you are obeying Murphy's Law! Murphy's Law says:

If anything can go wrong, it will.

When everything goes wrong at school or even on vacation, you know that Murphy's Law is at work. And who is Murphy? Edward A. Murphy worked with engineers on many projects. He always planned ahead and tried to think of all the problems that could happen. One day, while he was working, he made a comment about one of his workers, "If there is any way to do it wrong, he will find it." A manager on the project wrote down Murphy's idea and called it Murphy's Law. Now there are many sets of "Murphy's Laws" for different circumstances.

Here are some Murphy's Laws about travel . . .

- If the airline loses only one suitcase, it will be yours.
- If you get sick only once a year, it will be during your vacation.

. . . and here are some Murphy's Laws about school.

- When you're late for school, you'll meet the principal in the hall.
- The test that doesn't count is the one you got the best grade on.

Can you think of any other Murphy's Laws?

Unscramble the sentence:
anything/you/When/are/to/happens/for/happen/prepared/nothing

11 Listen. Write the number.

 12 Listen. Read and chant.

Murphy's Trip

We went on a trip to rest and relax,
but I'm sorry to say these are the facts.
Because of the traffic, we arrived late.
And while we were running out to the gate,
our plane took off without a care,
leaving us and our suitcases there.
When we finally got to our hotel,
we had some problems there as well.
While Dad was trying to pick up the key,
someone grabbed his cash and I.D.
So we slept in the lobby until half-past ten,
and then went right back home again.

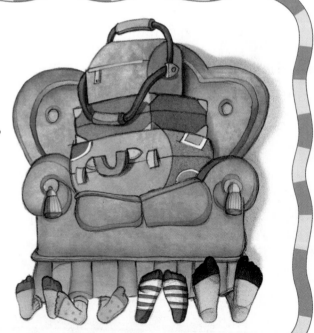

Project

Tips for Safe Travel

Make a poster. Draw a story to show an important tip for safe travel.

Play a Game!

What were you doing when it began to rain?

I was flying my kite.

✓ **KNOW IT? SHOW IT!**

What was the weather like last month?

Make a weather calendar.

It was raining when I came to school that day.

60 Assessment

✔ **Write words.**

1. _____ 2. _____ 3. _____ 4. _____ 5. _____

✔ **Write _the best_ or _the worst_.**

1. We were sitting at the beach; it was sunny but not too hot.

   We were having a great time. It was _____ day of our vacation!

2. We were setting up the tent when it started to rain.
   It rained for the next five days.

   It was _____ vacation ever!

✔ **Complete the sentences.**

1. We _____ on the highway when it started to snow.

2. While she _____, the lights went out.

3. I _____ for another flight when the airport closed.

4. _____ they _____ at 7:30 this morning?

5. While I _____ my bike, I hit a rock and fell off.

6. We _____ our homework when the alarm bell rang.

What happened to you while you were traveling?

_____

_____

_____

_____

Out of Touch

I decided to write
my best friend a letter,
but then I decided that
e-mail was better.

I typed out my message,
but when I clicked *SEND*,
it bounced back to me.
It won't reach my friend!

The next thing I tried
was my mobile phone,
but there was no answer.
Maybe no one was home.

Keep in touch!

So I checked out the forecast
on the TV news station.
There was a bad storm
in her part of the nation.

Well, her phone line is dead,
and the modem's no better.
So while there's a blizzard,
I'll just write her a letter!

2 Listen. Read and say.

Charles: I'm here with Ms. Rivera, the organizer of last week's science fair. Ms. Rivera, did the science fair have a theme?

Ms. Rivera: Yes. The theme was communication. **Everyone** did a project about that topic.

Charles: Did **anyone** do a project about the Internet?

Ms. Rivera: Actually, **no one** did. But **someone** researched the invention of e-mail.

Charles: What was your favorite project?

Ms. Rivera: **Someone** did a presentation on Braille. I liked that project a lot. It was very interesting.

Charles: Did **anyone** win a prize?

Ms. Rivera: Yes, there was a grand prize for the best project.

3 Talk and stick.
Use *anyone*, *everyone*, *no one*, and *someone*.

4 Look and read.

Not all communication depends on language. Here are some ways we communicate without speaking.

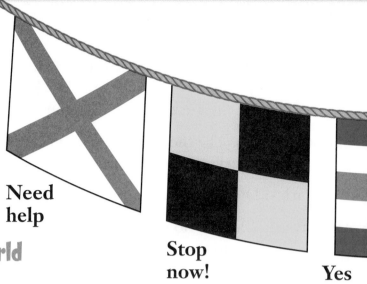

Need help

Stop now!

Yes

Body Language Around the World

Body language is a way to communicate using gestures, not words. Everyone uses body language all the time. Why? It helps us communicate. What do you think it means when someone puts his or her thumb up? What does it mean when you nod your head up and down? If you live in the United States, you will understand this movement means *yes*. But in parts of Europe it doesn't. Gestures for greeting people will certainly be different depending on where you are at the moment. How do you greet someone in your country?

A thumb pointing up means

- everything's OK (U.S.A.)
- the number five (Japan)
- looking for a ride (Canada)
- the number one (Germany)

Gymnast Mirna Tamiche gives a thumbs-up sign at the 2003 Special Olympics

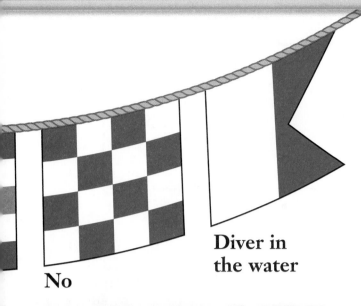

No

Diver in the water

International Marine Signal Flags

Sailors use international signal flags to communicate with each other and with people on land. There are 45 flags in all. Signal flags will always be useful because people can see them from far away and everyone at sea understands them. Each flag has a special meaning. If a ship shows the X flag, it means that it needs help.

Sign Language

How do you communicate if you can't hear or speak? Well, using your voice isn't the only way to communicate! Most deaf people use sign language. It is a way to communicate using special gestures instead of talking. There are different sign languages, just like there are different spoken languages. What do you think will happen if you use British Sign Language in China? People won't understand you! Many deaf people can also read lips and speak. Some experts think that all deaf people should learn how to read lips and speak so that they'll be able to communicate with hearing people. What do you think?

5 Point. Ask and answer.

Who uses body language?

Everyone uses body language.

6 Ask and answer.

Do you think people will continue to use body language?

Yes, I think they will. Body language will always help us communicate.

Grammar

What is she doing?	She's using the computer.
Where is the fax machine?	It's in the office.
When was the science fair?	It was last week.
Who will be at the library?	Our class will be there.
How do blind people read?	They use Braille.
How many signal flags are there?	There are 45.
How much does the newspaper cost?	It costs one dollar.

7 **Look at the picture. Write questions. Ask your partner.**

1. <u>What is the woman doing?</u>

2. _____

3. _____

4. _____

5. _____

Grammar

Will people continue to use mobile phones?	Yes, they **will**. People **will** always use phones.
	No, they **won't**. There **will** be a better way to communicate.

8 **Write questions or answers.**

1. Will people continue to use e-mail?

   Yes, _____

2. _____

   Yes, they will. People will continue to use Braille.

3. Will people continue to use stamps?

   No, _____

4. _____

   No, they won't. People won't watch television.

9 Work with a partner. Ask about a school event in the near future.

What school event can you tell me about?

The school play.

What is the event?	
When will it take place?	
Where will it take place?	
Who will come to the event?	
How long will it last?	

In the future, there will be flying cars.

10 Write predictions. Use these topics.

health   transportation   school   communication   food

1. _____

2. _____

3. _____

4. _____

5. _____

Share your predictions with a group. Rank them.

(1 = will definitely happen, 5 = will definitely not happen)

In Touch

INSTANT CHAT | **FUN AND GAMES** | **TAKE A QUIZ** | **FUN FACTS** | **GO SHOPPING**

Click here for

Catalan

Chinese

English

French

German

Japanese

Korean

Russian

Spanish

Thai

Urdu

CHECK iT OUT!

Talking gorillas? You bet! Koko the gorilla can use Gorilla Sign Language (GSL).

Who is Koko? Koko is an African gorilla. A scientist named Dr. Patterson taught her sign language.

What is GSL? Dr. Patterson wanted to teach Koko American Sign Language (ASL). But gorilla hands are not like human hands, so Koko had to change some of the signs. Also, gorillas use some of their own gestures to communicate with each other. GSL is a mixture of ASL and gorilla gestures.

Where does Koko live? Koko lives in California in a special forest with other gorillas. Scientists watch them to learn about gorillas.

When does Koko use GSL? She uses it when she wants to communicate.

Pretty cool! But if you go to a zoo tomorrow, the gorillas you'll see won't use GSL. Only Koko and her trained friends know this special language.

THIS WEEK'S OPINION:
Goodbye to Snail Mail!

In the future, no one will use "snail mail." Why not?

• Everyone will want to use the fastest method of mail. That's e-mail!

• No one will want to spend money on paper, envelopes, or stamps.

• Everyone will use a computer. It'll be easier to check your e-mail than the mailbox.

• The best reason: No one will have to practice handwriting in school!

What do you think?

Click here to chat.

FUN AND GAMES

What's black and white and read all over?
Unscramble the letters to answer the riddle.

P A R N W E E S P A

a newspaper.

Secret Communications

LEARN TO SPEAK IN CODE

A code is a great way to share secret conversations with your friends. Here's how:

1. Take the first sound in a word and put it at the end.

word ➜ ordw

2. Add *–ay* to the end.

ordw ➜ ordway

At'sthay oolcay!

BE A CODE BREAKER!
HOW? Read on to find out!

Now you can write secret letters with your friends!

1. Write out the alphabet.

2. Under it, write the alphabet again, starting with the letter *C*. Make sure each letter on top lines up with a letter on the bottom. The bottom is your code alphabet.

3 To write a message, use the code alphabet letters that line up with the real letters. The word *hide* will be *jkfg*.

4. Use the code to read a message. *Agu* means *yes*.

| REAL | A B C D E F G H I J K L M N O P Q R S T U V W X Y Z |
| CODE | C D E F G H I J K L M N O P Q R S T U V W X Y Z A B |

11 Listen. Write the letter.

1. ____
2. ____
3. ____
4. ____
5. ____

 (a)

 (b)

 (c)

 (d)

 (e)

 12 Listen. Read and chant.

We All Communicate

Exploring on the Internet
And having conversations
Learning from the media
Like news and TV stations
Calling on the telephone
Or sending out an e-mail
Mailing letters far away
Maybe using Braille
Using gestures all the time
Noting down a message
Introducing friends to friends
Creating a new language
And the list goes on and on
That no one can debate
Everywhere around the world . . .
We all communicate!

Project

LANGUAGE ARTS

Online Magazine

Plan a magazine for the Internet.

Will your magazine have sports biographies?

Yes, it will. Each week, I'll add a new biography about a sports star.

Taro's Sports Page

Do a Puzzle!

Work with a partner. Student A turns to page 111.
Student B turns to page 112. Give clues to your partner.

One across. What do you use to send e-mail?

A computer. Two down. How do blind people read?

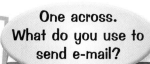

1. c o m p u t e r

People won't need to use sign language because scientists will make a hearing machine for deaf people.

✔ KNOW IT? SHOW IT!

Talk about communication in the past, present, and future. Make a chart.

Communication

Past	Present	Future
drums	snailmail email	mind mail
smoke signals	sign language	hearing machines

✔ Complete the sentences.

How can Tony and Koko communicate? They're using

(1) _____ to have a (2) _____.

The man and the gorilla both know the same (3) _____.

So when Tony has a (4) _____ for Koko, he knows

Koko will (5) _____ him.

conversation
gestures
message
sign language
understand

✔ Write questions.

1. _____ (What)

   I use the computer after dinner.

2. _____ (Who)

   Everyone in my family uses e-mail.

3. _____ (Why)

   Signal flags are useful because many people understand them.

4. _____ (How long)

   It takes three days to send a letter by snail mail.

✔ Complete the sentences. Use a negative if necessary.

1. In the future, we _____ stamps. (need)

   Everyone _____ e-mail. (use)

2. Next week, my teacher _____ us sign language. (teach)

   Then we can communicate without talking.

3. All gorillas at the zoo _____ GSL. (know)

   Someone _____ them. (show)

4. There _____ Braille numbers in all new elevators so
   blind people can use them. (be)

5. We _____ telephones. (have) We'll communicate in a different way.

How will we communicate in the future?

_____

_____

_____

Put on Your Thinking Cap

1 Read. Listen and sing.

How Do They Do That?

How do people think of things
like telephones and twine?
How do they get such great ideas
with brains like yours and mine?

How did we invent the wheel?
And was it made of rock?
How did people know the time
before there was a clock?

Who invented bars of soap?
That guy was pretty wise.
How did someone ever guess
hot air balloons would rise?

Who invented eyeglasses
and then the contact lens?
Who came up with crayons
or thought of ballpoint pens?

One day you might come upon
a problem you need to fix.
Just reach into your mind,
it's like a bag of tricks!

2 **Listen. Read and say.**

Grace: Look at that thing! What do you think it is?

Mitch: The front looks familiar. It might be some kind of television.

Grace: But look at the top. It's made of plastic and metal. And it looks like it's used to cook something.

Mitch: Well, it may be some kind of stove. Maybe it's a popcorn maker!

Grace: It might be. But look on the side. That part is made of metal, and it looks like a soda machine.

Mitch: You're right. This is really strange. I don't know what it's used for.

Grace: Do you think it might be used to do everything?

Mitch: What do you mean?

Grace: Well, it may be the perfect home-entertainment device. I think it might be a television with a built-in popcorn maker and soda machine!

Mitch: I bet you're right! What a cool invention!

What in the world is that?

It might be . . .

3 **Talk and stick.**

4 Look and read.

Learn about some interesting inventions.

Rubber Bands What a useful creation! In 1845, Stephen Perry made the first rubber band. Rubber bands are made of a special kind of elastic rubber. We use rubber bands to hold together papers, books, and other things. They have another great use, too! If you can't open a jar, wrap a rubber band around the top and then turn. The top will come off right away!

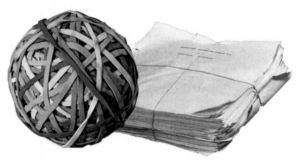

The Remote Control You use this plastic device every day to turn the television on and off and to change the channels. But the first remote control wasn't that convenient. It attached to the television with a big cable. People tripped over the cable, so no one liked this remote. In 1955, Eugene Polley invented a wireless remote. He solved the problem of the big cable, but his remote control had a new problem. It used light to control the television, and it didn't work very well on sunny days! Today's remote controls are much more advanced. In fact, some remotes can control several electronic devices at the same time.

Hot Air Balloons The Montgolfier brothers launched the first hot air balloon in 1782. It was made of paper. A year later, the Montgolfier balloon carried its first passengers—a rooster, a sheep, and a duck! Hot air balloons are still used to travel, to sightsee, and even to race. But today, they're made of cloth or rubber instead of paper. And they're certainly not used to transport farm animals!

5 **Point. Ask and answer.**

What are rubber bands made of?

They're made of elastic rubber.

6 **Ask and answer.**

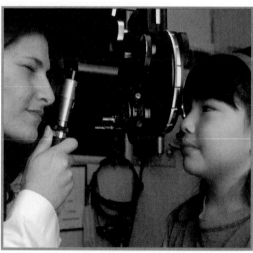

Contact Lenses Today, we use contact lenses to see better, and some people use them to change their eye color. The first contact lenses were made of heavy, dark glass. Then, in 1948, Kevin Tuohy made plastic lenses, but they were thick and stiff. In the 1970s, scientists created the soft plastic lenses many people wear today.

What are rubber bands used for?

They're used to hold things together.

What do you think it is?   I'm not sure. It **may** be something for the kitchen.

It **might** be a sewing machine.

7 **What do you think it is? Write two sentences about each item.**

1. _____   3. _____

   _____   _____

2. _____   4. _____

   _____   _____

What's it used for?   It's **used to change** the channel.

It's **used to hold** things.

8 **Write sentences. What's it used for?**

1. _____

   _____

2. _____

   _____

3. _____

   _____

4. _____

   _____

9 **Work with a partner.**

Student A uses this information. Student B turns to page 111.

What's it made of?	What's it used for?	What might it be?
metal		
	to have fun	
wood		
	to keep you warm	
glass		
	to communicate	

10 **Work with a partner. What different uses might each item have?**

plastic fork

_____

_____

_____

It might be used to protect your head from the sun.

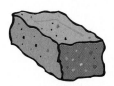

brick

_____

_____

_____

paper plate

_____

_____

_____

THINKING CAP

The Magazine for Creative Kids

Eleven-Year-Old Boy May Have the Solution!

How do you feel when you see an oil spill reported on television? Miro Keil, an eleven-year-old German boy, felt bad. After watching a big oil spill on the news, Miro came up with the idea to use liquid nitrogen to freeze the oil. He researched the subject and did experiments. Then he entered his idea in a science competition and won first prize. The judges thought Miro's solution was great. They told Miro to patent the idea! Who knows? Scientists may use Miro's idea to clean up the next oil spill disaster. Good job, Miro!

GUESS WHAT THIS IS!

Sonia Kumar's invention

○ a homework machine

○ a pet feeder

○ a bike washer

○ a map maker

A Happy Accident
A Delicious Discovery Becomes a Patented Invention

Popsicles are those frozen treats on a stick that we all love. An 11-year-old named Frank Epperson invented the popsicle by accident in 1905. One cold night, he left a fruit drink outside. The drink had a spoon in it. The liquid froze, and in the morning he had a new treat. In 1923, Epperson got a patent on his invention. Now, we enjoy popsicles that are made of fruit juice, cream, and chocolate.

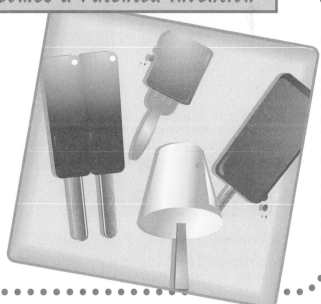

Coming Next Month

Ten Things You Can Do with Tin Cans

UNSCRAMBLE THE QUOTATION

INVENTION / NECESSITY / THE / IS / OF / MOTHER

—George Farquhar (1678-1707)

Listen. Write the number.

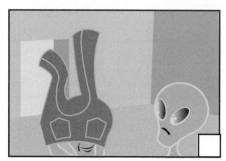
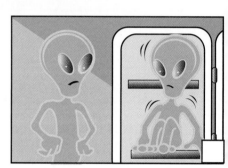

12 **Listen. Read and chant.**

In Trouble Again

I am an inventor and this much is true.
I invent things. How about you?

Once I invented a washing machine
that washed all my clothes until they were clean.

The best thing about this convenient device
was washing my clothes while riding a bike.

I liked my machine. I thought it was fine.
But I used some things that weren't really mine.

Don't use others' things, unless they agree,
or there will be trouble. Take it from me!

Project

Inventions

Use different materials to create an invention.

This raincoat is used for protecting your backpack.

What's it made of?

Plastic, wood, and cloth.

PLaY a GaMe!

Cut out the cards on page 121.

✓ KNOW IT? SHOW IT!

Take an object from the grab bag. Describe three ways it might be used.

✔ **What are they made of? Write words.**

1. _____ 2. _____ 3. _____ 4. _____ 5. _____

✔ **Complete the sentences.**

1. Windows _____ glass.
2. My jacket _____ cloth.

✔ **Complete the sentences. What are these items used for?**

change	hold	keep	see	travel

1. Contact lenses _____
2. Remote controls _____
3. Refrigerators _____
4. Rubber bands _____
5. Hot air balloons _____

Talk about a favorite object. Tell what it is used for.

_____

_____

_____

_____

UNIT 8 Product and Process

Stuff

Have you ever wondered
about all the stuff we use?
How we produce plastic
or get leather for our shoes?

Some things come from animals.
Some products are grown.
Some things we produce ourselves,
and some are made of stone.

Silk is made by little worms,
and rubber comes from trees.
Diamonds come from diamond mines,
and honey's made by bees.

Wool is cut off fuzzy sheep,
and cotton comes from plants.
Wool and cotton both turn into
blankets, skirts, and pants.

Whether things are made or grown
in Russia or Peru,
I know no matter where they're from,
I'll try them out—won't you?

Listen. Read and say.

1. The small clock is as expensive as the tall clock.
2. The blue album is as cheap as the red album.
3. The pink vase is as beautiful as the green vase.
4. The painting on the right is as modern as the painting on the left.
5. The small shirt is as colorful as the big shirt.
6. The doll is as old-fashioned as the toy train.

3 Stick and say.

④ **Look and read.**

Most countries in the world are known for both natural resources and man-made products of different types.

Costa Rica (Central America)

Costa Rica is known for its beautiful rain forests. They cover about a third of the country. Much of this land is protected by a land conservation program. Rare and beautiful wildlife, plants, and trees are found in the Costa Rican rain forests. But Costa Rica isn't only for scientists and tourists! Agricultural crops, such as coffee and bananas, are grown there and exported to other countries. Also, salt is produced from seawater.

China (Asia)

China is known for its many products, its large population, and its long history. More rice is grown in China, more steel and textiles are produced in China, and more people live in China than in any other country in the world. It is also a very big exporter of tea. The Chinese are known for inventing many useful and common things we use today, such as paper, gunpowder, silk, and the compass. One of China's most famous attractions is the Great Wall. It is located in northern China.

Italy (Europe)

Italy is known for many things, including fashionable clothing, modern furniture, beautiful glasswork, marble, and many historical and cultural attractions. Tourists come to Italy every year to see the sites and go shopping for popular Italian products like shoes and pottery. Foods such as olive oil, wine, and cheese are produced in Italy and exported abroad. Also, plenty of fish are caught and processed in the coastal areas of the country.

5 Point. Ask and answer.

What is Costa Rica known for?

Costa Rica is known for its beautiful rain forests.

6 Ask and answer.

Are there any well-known products from Costa Rica?

Costa Rican coffee is well-known.

Grammar

Indian tea is **as delicious as** Chinese tea.
The green vase is **as expensive as** the pink vase.

The green vase **isn't as expensive as** the red vase. (The green vase is cheaper.)

⑦ Write sentences.

1. Chinese cotton / soft / Italian cotton.

   _____

2. Dark chocolate / sweet / white chocolate.

   _____

3. Chinese gold / beautiful / South African gold.

   _____

4. Colombian coffee / popular / Costa Rican coffee.

   _____

5. Silk clothing / not / warm / wool clothing.

   _____

Grammar

Hollywood **is known** for its movies.
Italy and China **are known** for their delicious food.

know → known

⑧ Complete the sentences.

| catch → caught | grow → grown | know → known |
| design → designed | mine → mined | |

1. China _____ for the invention of fireworks.

2. Emeralds _____ in Colombia.

3. Rice _____ all over the world.

4. Fish _____ in the ocean.

5. Modern furniture _____ in Italy.

9 Work with a partner.

Student A uses this information. Student B turns to page 112.

What product is Canada known for?

Canadian lumber is well-known.

Country	Product	What is it?
Canada		Canadian lumber
Venezuela		Venezuelan emeralds
France		
Germany		a German car
Japan		
Mexico		Mexican weaving
Russia		
South Africa		South African diamonds
Turkey		

10 Work in a group.

What natural resources and products is your country known for? Make a list.

DeSoto Falls
fruit (bananas, mangoes)
jewelry

Do It Yourself Magazine

When you want the job done right, do it yourself!

Make Delicious Ice Cream at Home!

1. You need 2 cups of cream, 1 egg, 1/2 cup of sugar, and 1 teaspoon of vanilla.

2. All the ingredients are placed in a small coffee can. The top of the can is taped shut so nothing can spill.

3. The small can is put inside a larger can with ice and one cup of salt. The top of the larger can is also taped shut so nothing spills.

4. The large can is rolled back and forth for 15 minutes.

5. The large can is opened and the ice is poured out. The small can is opened and the cream mix is stirred. Then the whole process is repeated again.

6. Finally, the ice is poured out and the small can is opened. Serve the fresh homemade ice cream right away!

Happy Birthday, Mom

Guess who wrapped the present?

You did it yourself!

How did you know?

Did You Ever Wonder?

How do they get the stripes into striped toothpaste?

1. A small slotted tube is placed in the opening of a larger tube.

2. The long part of the tube is filled from the back with white paste.

3. The small tube is filled with colored paste.

4. The tube is squeezed and pressure is applied to the white paste.

5. Pressure is applied on the colored paste by the white paste.

6. As the white paste comes out of the tube, the colored paste is forced onto the white paste through the slots.

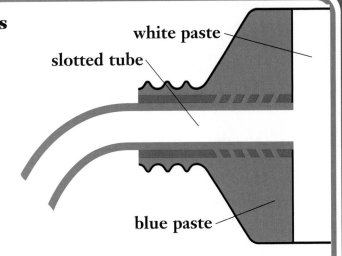

white paste

slotted tube

blue paste

Make Your Own Toothpaste

✓ It tastes as good as the toothpaste you buy at the store!

✓ It isn't as expensive as commercial toothpaste!

✓ Here's how to make it!

6 teaspoons baking soda

1/3 teaspoon salt

4 teaspoons glycerin

15 drops peppermint extract

Mix ingredients well to the consistency of toothpaste. Store in a container. Your mouth will feel very fresh!

WORD PUZZLE

Why should we give you the words? Find 11 more products yourself!

T	R	A	F	V	R	T	I	B	O	U	P	L	C	T	S	W	E	G	L	A	S	S	D
E	U	S	C	A	E	R	S	A	L	T	O	F	O	R	I	C	E	M	E	Y	T	I	U
A	L	A	O	B	L	G	O	L	D	S	T	W	T	E	C	H	A	M	A	R	B	L	E
E	R	V	F	I	V	H	L	A	F	R	T	A	T	N	T	U	W	I	T	Y	P	K	I
S	A	T	F	L	E	J	V	N	E	F	E	I	O	S	T	I	O	O	H	P	A	R	N
D	S	T	E	E	L	K	E	A	R	E	R	R	N	F	I	Y	O	F	E	A	I	Q	U
A	F	Z	E	N	O	T	R	S	M	O	Y	D	S	C	O	S	L	S	R	Y	R	X	A

Listen. Write the number of each step in the box.

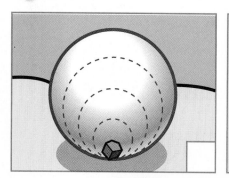

 Listen. Read and chant.

From Around the World

Where do we get it? Where is it sold?
From China and Russia come silver and gold.

How do we get it? Where does it grow?
It's Mexican coffee, didn't you know?

How do we make it? What's it made of?
Leather from Italy makes a fine glove.

Where does it come from? How is it used?
A Chinese toy keeps children amused.

Where do we grow it? What's it used for?
We can buy Indian tea at the store.

How is it played? Where is it from?
Show me that wooden Nigerian drum.

We make and export products to share.
And those we import come from everywhere.

Project

A Report

Prepare a report about a country and what it is known for.

PLay a GaMe!

Clara is as friendly as Barbara.

Start

the names of two friends

your shoes and your partner's shoes

the names of two sports teams

the titles of two movies

the names of two singers

two school subjects

your hair and your partner's hair

the names of two movie stars

the names of two cities

your English and your partner's English

End

 KNOW IT? SHOW IT!

Take an item from the grab bag. Talk about it.

This says "Made in India." It's used for jewelry. It's an Indian jewelry box.

GRAB BAG

✔ Complete the sentences.

Made in Korea   Made in Mexico   Made in China   Made in Italy

1. It's a _____ drum.

2. It's a _____ sweater.

3. It's _____ tea.

4. They're _____ boots.

✔ Write sentences.

1. South African diamonds / expensive / South American diamonds.

_____

2. Pearls / beautiful / emeralds.

_____

3. These cotton shirts / colorful / those silk shirts.

_____

4. The toy train / old-fashioned / doll.

_____

✔ Complete the sentences.

1. Ice cream _____ with cream and sugar.

2. Fish _____ off the coast of Japan.

3. Gold _____ in China.

4. Tea _____ in India.

Write about a country you know.

_____

_____

_____

And the Beat Goes On

1 Read. Listen and sing.

Sampling

Hey, I'm Dynamite Dan,
the DJ man.
Here to rap a beat,
so you'll move those feet.

Let's hear a taste,
no time to waste,
of what's in store.
Have you heard <u>this</u> before?

Get down with reggae.
What do you say?
This Jamaican band
is rockin' the land.

Now merengue's the beat.
It sounds so sweet!
What a happy sound.
Let's turn around.

Now check this out,
'cause without a doubt,
some good rock and roll
will move your soul.

You dance so well,
and I can tell
when you do your thing
that rhythm is king.

Listen. Read and say.

Andrea: Did you watch the *International Talent Show* on TV last night?

David: Yeah, I did. Did you see those two piano players? Weren't they terrible?

Andrea: Yeah, they played pretty badly.

David: I liked the guitar player though. His fingers moved so quickly! I hope I can play that well one day.

Andrea: I also liked the drummer with the green hair. She rocked!

David: Oh, yeah. She played so loudly!

Andrea: That was cool.

David: You're right. But the best was the duo that sang the love song.

Andrea: I know. They sang so beautifully. Some people in the audience even started to cry.

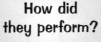

How did they perform?

 Talk and stick.

4 Look and read.

**People in all cultures love music.
There are many types of music.**

Rap

Rap music started with African
Americans in the United States, but
these days it's popular throughout the
world in countries as different as Spain,
Japan, Saudi Arabia, and Korea. In rap
music, performers talk to the rhythm of a
beat. Sometimes they use rhyming words
to make the rhythm clearer. I like it when
rappers talk quickly to match or contrast
the background beat. Sometimes I can't understand what
they're saying, but it sounds cool anyway. I've heard many
different styles of rap.

Steel Drums

Have you ever seen a steel drum
band? They play all kinds of music,
like jazz, reggae, and classical. Steel
drums come from Trinidad in the
Caribbean. A long time ago, people
there used metal objects like pots
and pans to make simple drum
music. In the 1940s, a 12-year-old
boy named Winston Simon made a
pan that could play different notes.
Other musicians quickly copied and
improved his instrument. Pretty
soon, steel drums were known all
over the world.

Salsa

My favorite kind of music is salsa. Salsa is a dance rhythm that has roots in musical styles of Cuba and Puerto Rico. It's the kind of music that makes you want to dance, especially when a Celia Cruz album is playing. I live in Japan where, believe it or not, we have several hot salsa bands. Some of us would rather listen to salsa than to traditional Japanese music.

Classical Indian

I like most kinds of music, but I'd rather listen to classical Indian music than anything else. Some Indian musicians play an instrument called a sitar. This instrument sounds beautiful when musicians play it slowly. When they play it quickly, the music is very exciting and lively.

5 **Point. Ask and answer.**

Have you ever heard rap music?

Yes, I have.

6 **Ask and answer.**

Would you rather listen to rap music or steel drums?

I'd rather listen to steel drums.

Grammar

Have	you they	ever **heard** salsa music?	Yes, I have. No, I haven't. Yes, they have. No, they haven't.
Has	he she	ever **been** to a music concert?	Yes, he has. No, he hasn't. Yes, she has. No, she hasn't.

7 Complete the questions. Then answer with your own information.

gone	heard	listened	played

1. _Have_____ you ever _listened_____ to rap music?   _Yes, I have._____

2. _____ your friends ever _____ to a concert?   _____

3. _____ you ever _____ drums?   _____

4. _____ your teacher _____ of reggae music?   _____

Grammar

Would	you he she they	**rather** listen to opera or jazz?	I He She They	**'d rather** listen to jazz.

8 Write answers.

1. Would you rather go to a concert or buy a CD?

   _I'd rather buy a CD._____

2. Would Luis rather sing songs or write songs?

   _____

3. Would they rather listen to music or dance?

   _____

4. Would she rather play the guitar or the violin?

   _____

9 **Interview your classmates.**

Find a different student for each picture.

Have you ever played drums?

No, I haven't.

10 **Work in a group. Which singers or groups would you rather listen to?**

Really?

Me, too.

I love pop music. I'd rather listen to Shakira than anyone else.

Teen Tunes
The Music Lover's Magazine

Spotlight on . . .

The Colombian Dynamo

Today, she's one of the hottest pop stars around. But how does this talented songwriter and musician make such great music? Shakira says that her music is a mixture of the things that are important to her and experiences she has had. This superstar sings in Spanish and English, and she performs incredibly well.

Shakira was born and raised in Colombia, South America. Her father is Lebanese and her mother is Colombian. She wrote her first song when she was 8 years old. She had her first recording contract when she was 13.

Shakira admits that while growing up she preferred music by the Beatles and Led Zeppelin. Now she would rather write her own songs. Some might say her music is a mixture of Latin pop, traditional Arabic music, and rock and roll. One thing is for sure: This spotlight star continually makes excellent music that becomes popular around the world!

How Much Do You Know About Music?

Match the artist and genre.

♪ Willie Nelson   Pop

♪ Louis Armstrong   Rap

♪ Placido Domingo   Country and Western

♪ Eminem   Salsa

♪ Yo-Yo Ma   Rock and Roll

♪ Celia Cruz   Jazz

♪ Kuraki Mai   Classical

♪ The Rolling Stones   Opera

NAME THAT TUNE!

THIS WEEK'S LYRICS

"They may say I'm a dreamer, but I'm not the only one . . . ."

Send in your response. Win a concert ticket.

AROUND THE WORLD: KOREAN DRUMMERS

Korean drumming is one of the most exciting varieties of music. In ancient times, drumming traditionally happened at farming festivals to celebrate planting and harvesting. Nowadays, drummers also perform on stage. They perform enthusiastically, with lots of movement and noise. Some of the drummers wear special hats with ribbons on them. While they are playing the drums, they dance around in circles and twirl the ribbons.

How is your musical intelligence?
Try our puzzle!

Across

2. Louis Armstrong's instrument
5. a mouth organ
6. a stringed instrument that stands on the floor
7. It has buttons and folds.
8. a tube-shaped instrument held to the side

Down

1. Bang on the _____.
3. instrument with black and white keys
4. It's shaped like a circle, and you shake it to make noise.

accordion	harmonica
cello	piano
drum	tambourine
flute	trumpet

This Week's Winning Joke
sent in by Sun-mi Lee

Q: How do you fix a broken tuba?

A: With a tuba glue.

On that note...
What's This?

Listen. Write the letter.

1. _____
2. _____
3. _____
4. _____
5. _____

 (a)

 (b)

(c)

 (d)

 (e)

Listen. Read and chant.

Have You Heard?

Aki plays the bongos.
Have you heard? Have you heard?
Aki plays so loudly that no one can hear a word!

Paula plays the piano.
Have you heard? Have you heard?
Paula plays so softly that a microphone's preferred.

Mei-Li plays the flute.
Have you heard? Have you heard?
Mei-Li plays so sweetly that it's like a singing bird.

Gary plays the guitar.
Have you heard? Have you heard?
Gary plays so terribly—it really is absurd!

Project

Musical Instrument

Make and talk about a musical instrument.

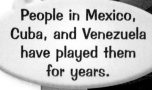

Play a Game!

Cut out the cards on pages 123 and 125.

The opera singer is singing loudly.

Right.

Most 13- to 19-year-olds would rather listen to rap.

✓ KNOW IT? SHOW IT!

Take a survey. Make a chart.

Ages	Classical	Rap	Reggae	Rock&Roll	Jazz
6-12				I	
13-19		IIII I	I	II	
20-26	I	I	II		
27-33	I			II	I
34+	I	I			

Do people of different ages like different music?

✔ **Write the kind of music.**

1. _____ 2. _____ 3. _____ 4. _____

✔ **Write questions. Use *would rather*.**

1. _____

I'd rather go to a dance concert.

2. _____

She'd rather listen to classical music.

3. _____

Twelve-year-olds would rather play the guitar.

✔ **Write questions or answers.**

1. Has he ever listened to opera?

No, _____

2. _____

Yes, they have. They went to a concert last month.

3. _____

No, I haven't. I want to take flute lessons next year.

 Write about two kinds of music you like. Which kind would you rather listen to?

_____

_____

_____

Unit 2   page 19 Student B

9 **Work with a partner.**

TV This Week		Saturday A.M.		
	Channel 2	**Channel 4**	**Channel 6**	
10:00		*Your Turn* game show (60 min.)	*Superduck* cartoon (30 min.)	
10:30	*Teen Talk* talk show (30 min.)			
11:00		*Amazing Animals* nature show (30 min.)		
11:30			*Children's Chorus* music (30 min.)	
12:00	*Spy Teens 3* action movie (2 hrs.)			

Unit 4   page 43 Student B

9 **Work with a partner.**

Discount Dave's
★★★
We have everything!
Check out these low, low prices!

$ _____

$129.95

$ _____

$8.50

Super discounts _____!

Stacy's
Department Store

BIG SALE this weekend!

Jewelry
$295.00

$135.00

Sweaters
$38.50

Footwear
$89.95

Unit 6 page 72 Student A

Do A Puzzle!

ACROSS

1. Used to send e-mail

6. How sailors communicate on the ocean

7. When having a conversation, you _____ and listen.

8. Hand and body movements used to communicate

10. The kind of phone that travels with you

11. Leave a _____ and I'll call you back.

13. Gestures that deaf people use are called _____.

Unit 7 page 79 Student B

9 **Work with a partner.**

What's it made of?	What's it used for?	What might it be?
	to eat food	
plastic		
	to keep things in	
cloth		
	to hold drinks	
paper		

Unit 6   page 72 Student B

Do A Puzzle!

DOWN

2. Blind people read using _____.

3. Secret ways to communicate in writing

4. There aren't any people in the room. _____ is there.

5. You can't use the phone now. I'm _____ the line.

6. The traditional mail system is called _____.

9. Gorilla language

12. Electronic mail on the computer

Unit 8   page 91 Student B

9 Work with a partner.

Country	Product	What is it?
Canada		Canadian lumber
Venezuela		
France		French cheese
Germany		
Japan		Japanese computers
Mexico		
Russia		Russian coal
South Africa		
Turkey		Turkish carpet

grandfather

cousin

sister

grandmother

nephew

uncle

niece

aunt

mother

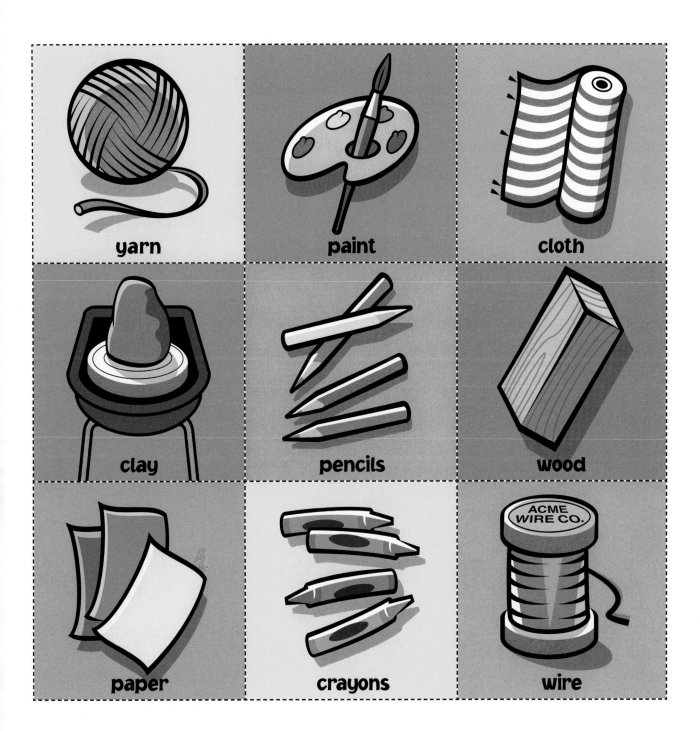

yarn

paint

cloth

clay

pencils

wood

paper

crayons

wire

loud → loudly

careful → carefully

beautiful → beautifully

bad → badly

quick → quickly

terrible → terribly

angry → angrily

quiet → quietly

happy → happily

slow → slowly

Grade 5 Stickers

Unit 1

Unit 2

Kim	Pat	Bill
Dan	Sue	

Unit 3

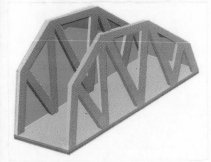

Unit 4

Unit 5

Unit 6

everyone **someone** **no one** **anyone**

Unit 7

   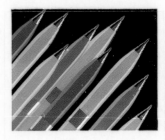

Unit 8

Unit 9

badly **beautifully** **loudly** **quickly**